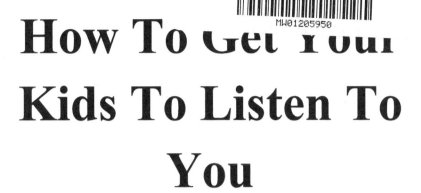

How To Get Your Kids To Listen To You

Communicating with Your Toddler, Tween, Teen and Older Children – Know How to Get Through to Your Kids

Jennifer N. Smith

Table of Contents

Introduction

It's the same story everywhere.

The moment your new baby home, theirs is the only voice to be heard anywhere. Your newborn would cry to get your attention, and your toddler would simply ignore your instructions. Your tween will start showing signs of rebellion and your teenager would dismiss any suggestion or advice that you might have. Even your grown-up children aren't much better, are they?

Kids never listen – that's the universal truth. It's not a comment on your parenting style, and certainly not your failure as a parent. You can have all the wisdom in the world stored in your brain, but your children would never want to listen to you. That's just the way it is with children and parents.

Trust me, I know.

My Story

Even just a few months ago, my home was a daily war zone. With a 6-year-old and a 2-year-old, someone would be screaming all the time. Either it would be me, my kids, or all three of us simultaneously. Not an hour would go by that someone wouldn't lose their mind, get frustrated and start to scream. As I was working from home at the moment, this would go on the whole day. My husband would come home from work to a screaming match, and it wasn't something he appreciated. Not day after day, after day.

To say that all our relationships were suffering would have been an understatement. Tired of screaming at the children all day, nagging and repeating myself, I wanted nothing more than a break at the end of the day. As a result, I would simply hand the kids over to my husband, who was tired from work, and vanish into the bedroom, excusing myself with a migraine. The kids, who had both scream like banshees all day and ignored all my instructions, would behave like little angels in front of my husband, just because they were missing him all the day.

Things got too complicated within a few months. My eldest, 6-years-old at the moment, had begun showing behavioral problems immediately after the birth of her sister. Overnight, she had become a jealous, malicious child from someone who was sweet tempered and disciplined. I had noticed the changes in her, but I was too busy taking care of my newborn child, my home, and my part-time job, to properly assess the situation. She stopped listening to me, started to directly disobey me, and even ignoring me at one point. As soon as my youngest reached her 2nd birthday, she started following her sister's behavioral patterns.

Suddenly, I was stuck with two children who, as it seemed to me, wanted nothing to do with me. I was their mother and they were practically ignoring me. My relationship with my husband, unfortunately, wasn't so great either. In such a small family, we were all basically resenting each other, minimizing our contact with each other. Personally, I was counting the days till they are grown up and I wouldn't have to deal with their day-to-day activities.

My Realization

One day, I suddenly decided that enough was enough. I wasn't having any more impertinence and disobedience in my home. I was missing out on the best years of my children's lives, and it was, to some extent, my own fault. Letting bygones be bygones, I was determined to make my kids listen to me and bring back some order into my home, whatever it took.

My Journey

I started researching parenting techniques. I must have bought tens of dozens of parenting books and gone through a million blogs on the articles. I talked to my friends who had children, to the other moms at my kids' schools, and even asked my mother, grandmother and aunts for advice. I asked, unabashedly, for advice to help my situation. I laid down all the facts out to them and asked them their expert opinion on how to approach my kids. Some of the advice I got was gold!

We all have different parenting styles and I wouldn't say I agreed to every advice I got. But I noted down every single advice that made sense to me, and decided on the ones I would apply in my family. I had a whole outline made, my take on each approach that I would use on specific situations.

I did, and – although it took time, they worked. No, it wasn't a miracle. I didn't say anything so special that my kids started to take notice of me immediately. It took weeks, even months, before I could get through the day without screaming. But after all the time and effort, I could finally get my children to notice me when I speak, listen to my words and follow my instructions.

It hadn't been easy, but I had finally learned to connect and communicate with my kids, and my relationship with my husband eventually improved, as well. My eldest is almost 7 years old now, and I couldn't have asked for a better child. It doesn't mean that she never rebels or disobeys me, but her tantrums have reduced drastically. My almost 3-year-old follows whatever her sister is doing, and is also being a model child. Most of the time.

Then, one day, I suddenly bumped into an old classmate at a coffee shop. She was alone but I had both my kids with me, thankfully, in a good mood. Watching them for a while, my friend exclaimed: ***"Wow! How did you get them to be so well behaved?"***

I wanted to take her through my whole journey at that very moment, but we didn't have the time. Instead, I made up my mind, then and there, to share my story with other parents out there who are also having trouble making their children listen to them. I decided to share my history with the other struggling parents and try to make their journey somewhat easier than mine was. That's how this book was born!

So. what can you find in this book?

This book is a compilation of everything I know about making your children listen to you. This is everything I have researched from the Internet, read in parenting books, heard from other parents and applied in my own family. I've divided this book into several sections, according to the age of the child you have to deal with. There's also a separate chapter at the beginning of this book which will help you to pinpoint the reasons behind your kid's behavior.

So, here's hoping my life experiences and my book can help you and your family to some extent. I would love nothing more than if I can bring a single kid and parent closer to each other with my s tory.

Thank you and good luck!

Communicating with Your Toddler, Tween, Teen and Older Children – Know How to Get Through to Your Kids

Chapter 1: Why Isn't your Child Listening to You?

You tell them to switch off the TV, only to still find them watching cartoons half an hour later.

You ask them to leave their dirty shoes outside, but find shoe marks all over your clean floor.

You nag and nag, all day, to finish their food, but all they do is to leave half-eaten bowls of cereal behind them.

You're tired of your kids not listening to you, no matter which technique you apply: bribing, threatening, blackmailing; nothing works. Your kids seemed determined to ignore you at all times, so much that you keep wondering if there's something wrong with them. Or with you.

This is not correct.

Remember, your children aren't being malicious on purpose. If they are being disrespectful, disobedient and disorderly, there's definitely some reason behind it. Just like kids throw temper tantrums, they sometimes choose to ignore their parents; there are usually some story behind their behavior, you can be absolutely sure about it.

I've compiled a few reasons that can make your kids ignore you. Some of them may apply to your family, although not all; these are just some of the reasons that make most children act out, rebel or disobey their parents, or whoever else is in charge of them.

Children Don't Listen Because they aren't meant to listen

This may sound weird to you, but children aren't meant to listen to you. They know you love them and care about them, but it doesn't compel them to obey you at all times. Just like adults, your kids would rather be doing what they love to do. Sometimes, they simply choose to ignore your instructions just because they'd rather do what's more interesting to them.

It's human nature to resist what someone else is asking you to do; your kids, although young, are just a human as you are. Naturally, they'll prefer to watch television instead of doing their homework. Wouldn't you rather stay at home sometimes and binge on your favorite TV series than go to work? So, can you blame your kids for something you've thought about often just because they don't understand social norms, rules and regulations yet?

Every kid thinks they are the ones in charge, so it's not surprising that they choose to ignore you sometimes. It's in their nature to resist what you are trying to tell them, just like adults often resist advice, criticism and guidance from others. It is the parents' job to find the balance between resistance and acceptance.

Children Ignore your Tone, not your Words

If your kids are choosing to ignore you, if may be because they don't like the tone you are using. Parents, naturally, get frustrated when they are not being heard and before you know it, you are screaming at your kids. It may start as something extremely simple, but at one point of the argument, you might start screaming at your kids. This is exactly when things will start to get downhill in your home.

The more you scream and shout, the less your kids are going to pay attention to you. They may respond to your shouting in a number of ways – by shouting back, getting angry, getting defensive or by turning defiant. In most cases, they might simply withdraw in their own shells and completely turn deaf, a fact that aggravates and frustrates parents more. The angrier and louder your tone, the less chances of your kid listening to what you have to say!

Parents might think your kids will listen to you when you raise your voice but in almost all cases, it's what stops your children from paying attention to you. On the other hand, when you scream and shout regularly, it can have an opposite reaction in your kids: *they might only respond when you are shouting.* With such children, you'll always have to scream to get things done, and that's certainly not what you want happening in your family.

Children Don't Listen Because You Don't Listen

You can't expect your kids to listen to you if you *never* listen to them. Remember, children learn by watching you, not by listening to you. You can lecture them a thousand times about how they've "got to listen to you" but that will not help. What they will only remember is that you don't listen to them, and that's it.

Many times, children try to tell us something and we are neither in the mood nor have the time to listen to them. We brush off their opinions only to ply more instructions on them, and they remember this the next time. When you don't listen to them, they choose not to listen to you, because that's what they have learned – from you!

Children Hate Lectures All the Time

You might not be aware of it, but parents have a tendency of lecturing their children more than we need to. Lectures may work with peers, students and employees, but they don't work on children. When lecturing, you may drone on and on and your kids will simply choose not to listen to you. With teenagers and older children, you may also experience eye rolls and sighs.

When you are lecturing your children, they get bored because you are talking too much. You can't really blame them on this, can you? Kids have a really short attention span, even your teenagers and older children, and you can't really expect them to sit back and listen to your lectures patiently. They can be running away in the middle of your lecture or simply tune you out and do whatever pleases them.

Kids Don't Like the Words You Use

Sometimes, kids don't listen when they hear you using words they don't like; usually, these are words like **"Can't"**, **"Don't"**, **"Why"**, **"No"**, **"Never"** or **"If"**. These are the words that limit their options or challenge them, and they prefer to ignore these words. When you point your fingers at them and say **"You"**, they feel threatened and completely tune you out.

The words may vary from kid to kid, but children usually react adversely to negative words. If they hear you using words that threaten, challenge or scare them, they'll distract themselves with some other happier thoughts and stop listening to you.

Children Don't Listen When You Nag

No one likes to be nagged, and neither do kids. If you keep on repeating and reminding them to do something, they will get tired of it. As parents, we often have to remind our children to do something they keep forgetting, and it can certainly become tiresome after a while. It's not just adults who react negatively to nagging; even young children can soon get tired when you are nagging them, repeating the same instructions.

Children Don't Hear when they are Distracted

A distracted child is not going to hear you, let alone listen to you! Kids get distracted very easily; their minds could be miles away when you are talking, thinking about something completely different, too busy to pay any attention to you. You might go on and on about something, and they wouldn't have heard a single word.

Similarly, kids can also get deeply immersed in something, especially the television, electronic gadgets or even books. Talk to them all you want during that time, and they won't hear anything at all.

Kids Might just be Mischievous

Sometimes, when your kid seems to be ignoring you, it might be just because they are having fun. Kids can actually enjoy the reactions they get from you when they don't listen to you; whether you scream in frustration, chase them, stomp your feet or threaten them, they enjoy the whole thing. This is more common among toddlers and younger children, as they aren't really scared of consequences.

If your child is simply being mischievous by not listening to you, you will know this by the smirk on their face or the glint in their eyes. Laughter will eventually follow seeing you frustrated and angry, as well. It's in their nature for children to be mischievous even when you are serious, so you need to identify the situation.

Kids May Not Understand What's Expected of Them

When you've been nagging to your child about keeping their room clean, stop and ask yourself this, "Have I taught them to clean their room? Are they capable of this task?" In the magnitude of parenting, we often forget the limitations of our kids; it may also happen when you have more than multiple children of different ages. Your 7-year-old may be capable of doing something you're expecting your 3-year-old to do, and they can't.

Your Kids May Simply Not Understand you

Have you ever thought of the language you use with your kids? Your young children may just not be able to understand what you are saying or trying to say. Using sentences that are too long or words that are too hard will confuse them, and it might simply seem disrespectful to you.

Also, children don't understand sarcasm or double meanings. Tell them, "Why on Earth would I want two disciplined children when I have you two?" and they will not be able to understand your sarcasm, negativity or true meaning behind your words.

Kids Don't Listen to Someone they don't Respect

This may sound sad, but sometimes, kids don't actually respect their parents. If you have not been a good role model for your children, if they had seen you lie, cheat or be disrespectful of others, do something you've punished them for doing – they can't respect you enough. This is more common in slightly older children than in toddlers or kids below 8. If you have never been sympathetic to their needs or turned a blind eye to their opinions, they won't be able to respect you as a parent, and children choose not to obey anyone they can't respect.

Your Kids May Actually Not Hear Properly

Finally, if you think your kids are ignoring your instructions, it may just be because they have trouble hearing. A lot of children suffer from hearing problems from birth, or it might be because of any illness or accidents. They might actually have a hard time hearing your instructions and simply chose to hide the fact, and instead let you go on and on.

Of course, it might be something completely different with your children, but I've found these points to be quite reasonable. As you can see, most of the time when you think your kids are ignoring you, they are not being rude, insulting or malicious; they are simply being children – children with their own opinions and choices. As parents, you need to be the one to make them listen, using only the right techniques.

Chapter 2: Start Before it's Time

The right time to start would be before your kid has actually started to ignore you, which would be around when they are toddlers. Yes, these days, unfortunately, even your precious toddler can completely disregard your instructions.

A toddler is a child from age 12 months to 36 months; this is a baby who has just learned to walk and run, speak and is discovering the world around them. Toddlers are especially inquisitive little beings. There's not much they don't want to touch, hold, break or experience.

This very important time of their life is when parents have a hard time teaching babies what's harmful and what's not, what can be touched and what needs to be avoided, and what they shouldn't be going near. Toddlers have receptive memories; i.e. they can remember something you've told them if only they pay attention to you. At this point in their lives, your instructions are extremely important for them, but you'll also need to make sure they listen to you.

One of the most difficult things you have to ever learn in your life is to talk to your toddler, to tone and dumb down your words so that they'll understand. It doesn't come naturally to everyone, but you can perfect it with regular practice.

To get your toddler to listen to you, here's all you need to know.

Don't Shout. Ever.

You can't scream at your toddler, period. No matter how angry you are, how frustrated or how desperate, you cannot shout at them. The first few times that you scream at your toddler, you can scare them into submission. They'll do what you want them to do, but they'll comply because they are frightened of you.

After this happens a few times, your screams are going to become normalized for them. They will be automatically programed to listen *only when* you shout. That is one of the most harmful things you can do to your children, and at such an early stage, it can be catastrophic. So, never, ever scream or shout at your toddler because it never works.

Screaming at them will only make your toddler more and more frightened of you. They won't know why you are shouting at them, why you are shouting or how they can make it stop, but they are going to fear you. Every time you scream, you are only making your toddler scared and confused, and this can actually lead to nightmares. Your shouting will be doing much more harm to your sensitive toddler than you can imagine; so whatever you do, never scream at them.

Speak to them, not at Them

Your toddler needs you to speak to them whenever you want to communicate. Speaking at them or about them won't get their attention. When speaking to a toddler, you have to get their attention first, and then talk to them. Call their name as many times as you have to until you have their complete attention, and then tell them what you want to.

Use calm words and a gentle voice when you are talking to your toddler, even when you are frustrated or seething inside. They may not understand most of the words you are using, but they'll appreciate the calmness in your voice and try to listen. Your kid will understand it when you're talking directly to them, and they will try their best to concentrate on your words.

Get Down to their Level

When you are trying to talk to or communicate with your toddler, you have to do it by being as physically close to them as possible. You can't expect your child to listen to you and understand you when you are speaking from the other end of the room, can you? They don't have the attention span to understand you from afar, either.

When you want your toddler to truly listen to you, get down to their level and look them in the eyes. They need to see you looking at them and talking to them to completely comprehend your words. So, you have to either squat down to their level or pick them up in your arms to talk to them, or sit them opposite to you on a chair.

Use Their Name

You can call your child every adorable name under the sun but when you want their attention, use their name. Call them by their real name when you want them to listen to you properly; go on using their name until you have their full concentration.

Try this technique every single time you are about to place some instruction in front of them. A few times later, whenever they hear you call their name, your toddler will instinctively be ready to take down some form of instruction or order.

Look into their Eyes

This is actually the last of a manifold step: *come close enough to have physical contract, squat down to their level, use their name to get their attention, and then, make eye contact.* All these steps are absolutely necessary to get their full and unwavering attention. Don't talk to them until you have the attention you need, because your words will fall into deaf ears.

Eye contact is also important for toddlers for another reason. When you look into their eyes and talk, they learn new words. This is the technique you should also use when introducing new objects, terms and ideas to them - look into their eyes and say the word out loud.

Be Precise

Toddlers don't have a very large vocabulary; so, there's no need to use too many words with them. They will only start forming sentences between their second and thirds year, which means your instructions need to be as precise as possible.

You can talk to your toddler as much as you want any other time to build their vocabulary, but you need to be brief when you want them to understand. Use two-word or three-word sentences for your instructions; anything longer will simply confuse them. If you launch into explanations and long instructions, they would probably stop listening somewhat in the middle.

So don't say: *"It's so cold outside; you need to wear something warm! Come on, let's dress up really nicely with Mommy."*

Simply say: *"Time for a coat;"* you can explain the reasons for a coat later when they are putting it on, just to introduce new words into their vocabulary, but don't mix your instructions with explanations.

Don't Give Them Too Many Options

Even your toddlers understand what *freedom of choice* is, and you don't want to give them too many options. If you ask them: *"Do you think we have played enough, and that it is time for bed now?"*, of course they are going to choose to play some more. Give them the option between a bar of chocolate and a fruit, and they are going to want the chocolate, surely.

You have to be a little strict when you want your toddler to listen to you and do what you want them to do. Instead of giving them the choice between 'going to bed and playing', say *"Time for bed"*. It might take them a few minutes to actually give up playing and get ready for bed, but you have to be patient.

Be Animated in your Instructions

Don't just use your words when giving them an instruction, but your eyes, your hands, your mouth and your entire body. Don't just say "cold" or "hurt" or "yummy", make the necessary gestures. When you say *"Wear your coat, it's so cold outside"*, make shivering motions with your body and say, *"Ooh, cold!"* This will make the instruction more interesting to your toddler, and they will gradually start to associate 'cold weather' with 'wearing a coat'.

In the same way, rub your belly when you say *"Yummy banana"* or make a sad face when you say **"Booboo!"** Your toddler will appreciate the visual lessons as well as the words you are using.

Don't be Too Strict

You might be the parent and know what's best for your toddler, but that doesn't mean you have to be strict about everything. Give them some wiggling space at times; otherwise, they will become wary with you always ordering them around.

Five more minutes of playtime won't hurt if you see your toddler is really enjoying something; a slightly late-night tuck in should be allowed at some time. Be strict with your toddler when it comes to their wellbeing, but you can afford to let go at times, too.

Though your toddler is not old enough to understand what's good for them and what's not, they are old enough to know what they enjoy doing. Leave them alone to their enjoyment sometimes, because that's how they'll learn to grow.

Be Realistic in your Expectations

You might love it if your toddler can keep their playroom neat and pick up after themselves, but you really can't expect them to. But, you can expect them to help you. Keep in mind what your growing toddler can and cannot do, and mellow your instructions as per their age.

Don't just tell them to **"clean up the room"**; instead make it into a game with you. Ask them to **"gather all the dolls around"** or **"collect all the blue Duplo pieces"** and help them with the task.

These are the years that your child should learn basic housekeeping skills, but only if you are realistic about everything.

If you instruct your two-year-old to dress themselves – something they are probably not capable of doing, no amount of shouting or threatening will make the job easy for them.

Give Appropriate Praise

Give them their due praise and reward when they are due. If your fussy toddler finishes eating without a tantrum, shower them with *"What a good girl/boy!"* and *"There's my wonderful little baby; what a great girl/boy she is!"* comments.

Your toddler will truly appreciate praise from you, especially if they are accompanied by a few kisses. They are not yet ready for "You'll eat your breakfast if you are a good baby" logic, but they'll understand your happiness after a job well done, and you can bank on that.

Follow Through your Directions

Once you've asked them to do something, follow it through. If they want chocolates for lunch, don't say *"Not before you've finished your food"* only to give in a few minutes later. *"Drink your water"* means that your child needs to drink water at that moment, or even 5 minutes later, but don't give up and say *"Okay, fine; I'll get you juice"* if they want a substitution.

The main agenda is that you need to be the strong one in the relationship. Your toddler can't know that you'll give in to their request if they cry, whine or start a tantrum. If this is something they really, really want, you can allow a chocolate *after they've finished lunch* or *juice after they've drunk their water,* but you shouldn't go back on your words just because your toddler is being bossy.

Say "No" the Right Way

Although there's no direct harm in it, many parents prefer not to say "no" or similar negative words to their toddler. According to pediatric psychologists, too many limitations and too much of hearing "No" can actually desensitize a child, make them unwilling to experiment or take risks later in life. Besides, when you tell them "not" to do something too much, they might just get rebellious. Therefore, while you may actually have to utter the words "No" and "Don't" a few times, there are ways to avoid them.

Here are some other ways to get your toddler to stop doing something without actually having to say "no".

- **Too much isn't good for you.** When your toddler wants to binge on chocolate or play for a long time, this is what you can say without using the words **"no"** and **"don't"**.

- **Let me show you.** Instead of stopping them with negative words, correct them with actions.

- **Let's be.** Stopping your toddler to hit, bite or fight doesn't require you to use the words "no". You can simply say "Let's be friends" or "Let's be kind".

- **We use our words.** Another great way to stop fighting between siblings; tell them to "Use their words instead of their hands".

- **Use your regular/normal voice.** It's frustrating when your toddlers whine, cry or shout. Instead of saying "Stop" or "Don't", try saying "Tell me in your regular/normal voice".

- **"Stop!", "Hot!", "Ouch!" or "Danger!".** The moment you see your toddler about to touch something dangerous, the first word you instinctively utter is "No!". If this is something you want to avoid, you can try the ones highlighted above.

Give Them Plenty of Attention

The more attention you give your toddler, the more attention and good behavior you'll get from them. Very often, a misbehaving toddler is only looking for your attention, and nothing else. Have you ever caught your toddler doing something you've especially asked them not to, a thousand times over? They may just be feeling lonely and need your company, and misbehaving is the fastest way to get attention.

When this happens, what they need is some attention, not discipline. When you give them some company and affection, it will be easier for them to listen to you.

Give It a Break

Sometimes, you've been telling your toddler that it's time for bed, but they are just too busy playing than listen to you. In these situations, we simply start yelling, force them to come with us, or start nagging, repeat the same thing again and again, until the whole situation worsens. The right thing to do, instead, would be to simply take a break.

If your toddler seems pretty absorbed in their game, let them play for some time. Another 10 or 20 minutes isn't probably going to do much harm to your day, unless you are going out. Take this time to grab a cup of coffee or read a few pages from the book you've been meaning to finish, or even participate in the games with your child, until they are ready to go to break.

Be a Good Listener Yourself

To have a good toddler in the house, you need to be a good role model yourself. If you want your toddler to pay attention to you and listen to you, you must also listen to them.

Granted, there's nothing really interesting that a toddler can tell you, even if they can finish a full sentence. However, anything they want to tell you, show you and share with you, is interesting to them. You have to show them that you are interested in them by paying them the attention they thrive on. Play with them, listen to what stories they have to tell, what they have to show you, and everything they want to share with you. If you dismiss their need to spend time with you and limit your relationship to only directions and instructions, can you really expect them to pay attention to you as they grow up?

Above everything, what you need to remember is that you are dealing with an adorable toddler here. Even when they frustrate or anger you, they are not doing it on purpose. Being rebellious is just a part of growing up, and every toddler goes through almost the same phases. At the same time, if you don't make your toddlers listen to you, you are going to have more problem later.

Your toddler needs your love, attention and care more than they need disciplining. Start small when they are toddlers, so that you neither limit their mental growth nor let them go wild with too much independence.

Chapter 3: Ages 4 to 8: Time to Get Serious

This is the difficult age when children can start to get on your nerves because sometimes, they'll simply refuse to listen to you. No reason, no back stories, no purpose – children in their 'late childhood', which is the psychological term for this age, loves to be difficult at times.

This is the age between their childhood and their tween years, and kids see a lot of changes in themselves during these few years. It is at this stage that you can see a glimpse of who your child is going to be when they grow up to be an adult.

Important Features of this Age

From ages 4 to 8, kids get the first taste of independence. Some of them start school for the first time and as a result, meets new people who aren't family. They learn something new every day, some of them good, but mostly bad. They want to experience new things, try new things, and hates being inhibited. If you are honest, this age is more difficult for them than it is for us parents.

There's a lot new that you can see in your kids at this age that they didn't have before. They'll need less sleep and rest, and will always have more on their minds. Kids first begin to understand the concepts of 'consequences', 'logic' and 'negotiations' at this age, so it is possible to talk to them.

Kids between ages 4 to 8 have a lot on their minds and very little time to listen to you. They would prefer to do something that appeals to their personality rather than what you want them to do. At this age, kids gradually start to come out of their parent's shelters, and the outside world might seem more interesting to them. Indeed, these are the years when you need to be a little strict with them; too much independence, and you will lose their obedience later during the tween and teen years.

When you know the tricks of this age, it can become a little easier for you to handle your 4 to 8-year-old kid, and get them to listen to you. Here's what you can try.

Use Single (or Double) Word Instructions

Your 4- to 8-year-old might have a larger vocabulary, but they also have a very short attention span. Instead of giving them long, rambling instructions that they will understand if only they pay enough attention to you, place all your authority on one (or two) word. You can say "It's lunch time; come and have your lunch now before everything gets cold" but you can't possibly say all of those words with the same weight.

So, instead of that long sentence, simply say *"Lunch"* or *"lunch time"* or even *"Food"*, and say that one word with a strong, powerful voice. Even if your kids can't understand your instruction the first time, they will from the next time.

Save your words and it will be peaceful for you, as well. Instead of using long sentences where you might practically end up whining or requesting, give the same instruction in one or two words.

Give them Some Information

Your kids are growing up, and they deserve more than just plain orders from you. Try to give them a little information every time you want them to do something or stop doing something; for example, if they are in the process of plucking out a flower from someone else's garden, tell them, *"Did you know flowers get hurt when you pick them from the tree? You might not hear it, but they will cry"* instead of a simple *"Don't pick flowers."*

Give them a 'why', 'when', 'what' and 'which' as you give them an instruction. Instead of saying *"Stop touching everything,"* say *"These things will break if they fall from your hands, and you will feel sorry then"*. Give them enough to think about and maybe question you later, because this is a great age to learn and discover new things.

Acknowledge their Emotions

Don't just assume your kids don't have any feelings or emotions in them because they are children. Children experience extremely intense emotions at times; they can be just as angry, frustrated or sad as adults. When you see your kid reacting to something, stop your instructions for a few minutes and try to empathize with them. Acknowledge that they too have feelings and you might just get them to listen to you.

Just imagine how you would feel if someone spoke to you the way we sometimes do with our kids? How would you feel if someone turned off the television in the middle of your favorite TV show, just because they think you need to take a nap? Children can feel the same way if parents are too bossy or too forceful. So try and understand their emotions, and they will, in return, listen to you.

Instead of saying, *"Enough TV! Turn it off right now and go to bed!"* try saying *"I know you're enjoying this show a lot, but it's bedtime. Do you think you can turn off the TV after this episode and we can go to bed?"* Your child will appreciate being treated like an adult rather than a child, and they'll listen to you because you've been fair to them.

Try sentences such as *"I understand you want to play some more, but…"* and *"I can see that you are upset, but…."*; your child will appreciate the effort.

Give them Trick Choices

Kids aged 4 to 8 would appreciate some choices, but you don't have to give the power back to them. You can give them some choices and give them the power to make decisions, but they need to be trick choices so that you ultimately get what you want.

Don't ask them whether they want to do their homework or watch television, because you know what they are going to choose. Instead, ask them: *"Do you want to start with your English homework or your Additions?"* Whichever your child chooses, they get to do homework, but with the satisfaction that they had taken the decision themselves. Don't ask them *"What do you want for a snack?"* and wait for when they ask for chocolates or a milkshake; ask: *"Which one do you feel like today – an apple or a banana?"*

Of course, there's always the chance for them to want a third option, but there are other ways to deal with that.

Don't Back Out

Try as much as you can to not back out from any of the instructions you give your children, however small. This might happen sometimes, but you need to minimize the times they do. Don't tell them to brush their teeth and then back out because you can't stand the whining and the complaining. Postpone the event for a few minutes if you need to, but don't back away completely.

If your kids see you backing away from your instructions every time they start to whine, they will make it a habit whenever they don't feel like brushing, doing their homework or drinking their milk. Do it only a handful of times because you don't want to seem like a tyrant either, but make the occasion memorable. Make it sound like it is a treat to be let off your instructions some times, but not something you are going to do often.

Give them Routines

A clever way to make sure your child does everything you want them to without having to use too many words is by giving them a routine. They need a specific routine in their life from the time your kids start school, just so that they can appreciate the idea of a well-structured day. You can start with a simple *"Pajamas-brushing-bed"* routine before tucking them in every night; with a few days of supervision, your school going child will learn to maintain order by themselves by following their routine. You won't have to go through the *"Did you change? Did you brush your teeth? Are you ready for bed? Is it time to come and tuck you in?"* questions. Just one word: *"Bedtime",* and your kid immediately know what is expected of them, what to do, and in what order.

Gradually, you can extend these routines to other parts of their day, such as: *"Brush teeth-wash face-brush hair-dress up-come to breakfast"* routine before leaving for school every day. They are going to need some supervision the first few days, but will automatically know to follow the routine later. Another favorite one of mine is the *"remove shoes-take down school bag-put bag and shoes in designated place-wash your hands-come down for a snack"* routine after coming home from school every day.

Start on Deadlines

At ages 4 to 8, your kids might not completely understand time, but you can still give them deadlines. Start with *"You can watch TV while the grown-ups finish dinner, but afterwards, it's bed!"* and *"You can play with your toys until I call everyone for dinner."* This way, they'll have time to prepare themselves for what's to come and will appreciate your warning, instead you coming in to ruin their fun time suddenly with an abrupt instruction. They might not understand all the time, or lose track of time, but many times, you can see that they are turning off the television or stop playing when you remind them that the deadline is here.

One Direction at a Time

Although they are old enough to understand long sentences, it's better you don't overdo with instructions. Give them single instructions in short sentences, wait for them to be completed, and then get on with the next set of instructions. Don't tell them to finish their homework, then put their books away, then tidy the table, and then to get ready for dinner. You can't really expect a child to remember everything you've told them to do and follow through.

Instead, tell them to finish their homework quickly; then, after they are done, ask them to put their books away, and so on. Wait patiently as they go through every single instruction to give them further ones instead of dumping them all on a 4-year-old or even an 8-year-old. You might have to check in again and again with their progress and repeat your instructions, but it is better than to dump a whole package of information on them and wait for them to fail.

Give Specific Instructions

Be specific when giving your instructions, even if you have to use dozens of words to get the work done. Don't tell them to clean up their room or to do their homework, because children aged 4 to 8 aren't that organized. Be extremely specific with them, such as *"Pick up all the clothes from the floor"* or *"Take out all the books from your bag".* Otherwise, with generic instructions, you'll end up with a confused kid who doesn't know where to start or exactly what to do.

Instructions such as *"Be good!"* also doesn't register very well with toddlers. If you want them to be well-behaved at the store or when company comes over, you need to give them specific instructions such as *"No touching anything"* and *"No screaming when people come over".* You might even have to repeat them a few times for your toddler to fully understand them.

Give Rewards and Praises

Never be stingy with rewards and praises when they deserve it; always remember to give a *"Well done!"* or a *"Thank you"* when they've been helpful or when they've been obedient. Children of this age love a visual representative of their life, so a sticker board or a star chart can be quite helpful. This might even be something they show off to guests, visiting cousins or their own friends, something for them to be proud about.

You can put in stars for every time they have been good all day, and if they make a specific number, they get a reward, such as breakfast of their choice, their favorite story for bedtime, or an extra hour of cartoons. Being good all week can mean a trip to their favorite playground or eating at their favorite restaurants, and such.

However, you need to remember to make these treats into rewards for good behavior, instead of bribes. Don't bribe them into good behavior, but give them rewards. There's a distinction between the two concepts that you need to maintain.

Let them Decide Sometimes

Not everything has to be about giving instructions and obeying them; sometimes, you can move away from the parent-and-child equilibrium. At times, it's completely okay to ask your kid what they want to do, and follow their plans.

This will create a balance in your relationship, if not anything else. Your child will remember that you do listen to them sometimes, and that will help them decide to listen to you. Besides, no relationship is equal where one person orders and the other one obeys all the time; you have to balance out the relationship sometimes and let your kid be in charge.

Finally, remember that this is a loving relationship you have with your child. This is not a relationship based on power or control, but one based on love. You give your kids instructions all day long to make them skilled for real life, but that's not your whole relationship.

At this age, your children need plenty of love and affection, showered on them every day. You need to show your kids you love them, both when they are behaving well or behaving bad. Ages 4 to 8 is when you need to discipline your kid, but also when you need to love and support them at all times. Growing up, all kids will be a little undisciplined, unruly and unmanageable. To completely mold your children would be to thwart all creativity and uniqueness, and this is not something you want.

Chapter 4: Talking to your Tweens, Making them Listen

Teenage comes early to kids of this age, and that is exactly why psychologists have discovered a new age group – the tween years. Anyone from ages 9 to 12 are a tween, just before they reach their teenage years. Just like a teenager is neither an adult nor a child, a tween is also in the middle of their childhood and their teenage years – a very confusing time for them.

Why are the Tween Years Special?

Teenagers aren't considered to be children anymore; rather, they are known as 'New Adults'. This makes the tweens the new teenagers of this era.

Parenting has changed a lot since we were kids. All our parents had to worry about were disciplining us, but now, many other concerns have entered the field. While parents of tweens have to deal with talking back, insolence and rudeness, the tweens themselves have to worry about social acceptance, bullying, mental and physical changes. It's not easy to either parties – this age; however, since the tweens are still the ones growing up and adjusting, it falls to the parents to help them through these difficult four years.

The tween years only last 4 years, from ages 9 to 12, but can feel like an eternity to parents. Most parents used to dread the teenage years, and now, the teenage years have come even closure.

Still, the tweens are a special time for your kids and for you. You can see firsthand your little kids growing up into something resembling a mini adult, with their own choices and opinions. You might have been able to talk to your child before, but you can finally carry on a decent conversation with your tween, adult-to-almost-adult.

You can talk to your tween, but making them listen to you can be tough. They are growing up into an adult themselves, and they can't be molded so easily in their tween years as they could be before. A child would follow your instructions because they knew they had to, but a tween can come back with a "Why" and a "Why not". More frustratingly, they can simply say "No", no matter how much it aggravates you.

So, here's everything I've learned about dealing with tweens.

Don't Shout

Even the most well-behaved tweens can be rude at times, making you frustrated and angry. However, the moment that you lose your temper is the moment that you lose the fight. No matter how angry or frustrated you are, you cannot start screaming, yelling or shouting at your tween.

Easier said than done, I know. But that's the way it should be. Your younger children might have been frightened by your shouting but your tween will only rebel back. Especially, you cannot yell at them to get them to do something.

If screaming does help, save them for serious occasions, when they have actually done something atrocious. Don't yell at your tween simply to go through the day, because it's going to make the matter worse.

Give Them Actual Reasons

When you're telling your tween to do something, or not to do something, give them some actual reasons rather than *"Because we know better!"* and *"Because we're the parents and you have to do anything we tell you to do!"* You are not trying to establish an autonomy in your home, are you? When you want your tween to obey your rules or stop them from doing something they want to do, they deserve an explanation.

"We can't go out for dinner tonight, because we have a one-restaurant-one-week rule in this house; we've already eaten out once this week. Next week, I promise we'll go to your favorite pizza place." Now, doesn't that sound better than *"We're not going to eat out tonight just because you feel like it. Now, don't bother me anymore and sit down quietly for dinner, and be thankful for it."* What do you think?

Also *"We can't get you that toy now because you know you only get one toy every month, don't you? I understand that you would really love to have it, but we're going to have to wait till next month to get it for you. You do understand that, don't you?"* instead of *"No more toys! You're always asking for toys when you know you only get one every month! Why don't you understand that? Why are you always pestering me about new toys? I said No!"*

Be gentle and understanding with them, and give them a good reason about why you are denying their requests – not because you are the parents and you have the power to do so, but because you have a good reason for it. They might still whine and pine away for what they wanted from you, but only for the first few times; then, they will try to use their newly matured brain to think about what you've told them.

Be Honest about your Limitations

When you abruptly deny your tween's requests or wishes without giving them a reason for it, it's going to break your child's heart. Sentences such as *"Don't ask me why, you won't understand"* or *"Whatever I say is right and needs to be followed at all times, no questions asked"* can seriously hamper their confidence in themselves. Your tweens actually have the capability of understanding more that you think, and by not giving them actual reasons behind your decision, you're insulting their intelligence.

Your 10-year old is capable of understanding your limitations and problems, but if you are honest about them. Suppose your family has just come back from a lovely holiday and now, your tween is pestering you about going to another one. It's understandable that you burst out and say: *"But we just came back from a vacation! You want to go to another one? Do you have any idea how expensive these vacations are? Have you got any idea how much we have to work to give you this life? Sometimes, you sound so spoiled! I just don't know what to do with you when you are so illogical."*

Imagine your kid's reaction to this! They haven't asked for anything illogical, have they? Even us adults long for holidays to go on and on forever, and kids only say out loud what we are all thinking. Instead of taking it out on them, you could try this track: *"Yes, that was a lovely holiday, wasn't it? I also wish we could go to another one, and we will, but in a few months. Mommy/Daddy has to work more and save money so that we could go to an even better hotel the next time, and you have to go to school. Everyone misses you at school, don't they? We also have so much to do at work, too. When we're ready again in a few months and have the money we need, we'll plan for another vacation soon. Do you understand?"*

You might think your tween is too young to understand about work and money, but they are not. By talking to them this way, you're giving them something to think about, and also something to look forward to. They'll pay attention to you more as a human being who has to work, save money, pay bills and plan for a vacation, rather than someone who is only there to fulfil their every whim.

So, if the occasion arises, talk to your tween about the serious things in life, such as obligations, financial limitations, responsibilities, etc. They'll understand; if they don't, they'll think about it.

Never Bribe, Threaten or Blackmail

They don't work and what's more, bribing, threatening and blackmailing your tweens will only increase the distance between you.

There's a thin line between *"If you behave well in this party, you'll get a new toy"* and *"Since you've been a good boy/girl all week, you've made us very happy. As a reward, you get a new toy this weekend"* that parents often mismanage. Rewarding positive qualities is good but bribery isn't; when you bribe your child for your own gain, i.e. good behavior at a party or n tantrum for the day, they'll learn to do the same to you.

Similarly, you can take away your child's privileges when they've been bad, but you can't threaten then with physical or mental punishments (*"I won't love you anymore"* or *"I'll not be sad if anything happens to you"*). Why? Imagine someone you love saying something similar to you. How would you feel if your partner said they won't love you anymore if you don't cook them dinner one day? Devastated, indignant, angry, disposable, vulnerable? Well, your child will be feeling exactly the same.

It's the same with blackmailing your child. Saying *"If you don't behave well when the guests arrive, I'll tell everyone what a naughty child you are!"* can be more harmful to them than you can imagine.

Threats, bribes and blackmailing may work in the short time, but your child will lose all their love and respect for you if you continue to make them all the time, and as we've stated before, children won't listen to someone they can't respect.

Be a Good Role Model

Children follow everything you do and say; before telling them to something, be sure you follow your own rules. You have to be a good role model for your child if you want them to be on your best behavior. Your tweens will understand you more than your younger children can, so you need to be more careful around them.

Think about this: can you tell your tween to stop wasting their time on the phone when you can be seen on the phone all the time? How can you teach them not to interfere when someone else is talking when you visibly do it to them? When you eat junk food, can you stop your kids from doing the same?

So, with tweens, you need to be the model for what you want them to be. If you want your tween to listen to you, you have to show them exactly how you want them to behave – not just tell them, but show them.

Tell them Stories about Yourself

Your tweens are at the stage where they'll soon start to roll their eyes at everything you say, but there's still time for that. For the tween years, there's a great technique to make them listen to you. Not to your instructions, commands or rules, but simply to your stories.

Just talk to them: tell them stories about your childhood, your school friends, your hobbies, your day, anything at all, as long as you continue to talk enthusiastically. Your kid might not even seem to be listening, but don't let that stop you from talking. Don't try to sneak in some kind of advice in your stories because your tween might see through it. Let this time simply be a bonding time with your kid, a short 20-minute session every day.

This might not be the type of listening that you want to learn about, but a simple bonding sessions is just what you need with your child. Your tween might pick up a lot from your stories, so be careful about the stories you are telling them.

Listen to Them

Just like you want your kids to listen to you, you need to listen to your tweens. Pretty soon they'll start to talk less and less, and keep secrets from you, so enjoy this time. When you talk to your tween, they'll want to talk to you as well, and this is when you need to listen.

If you're honest, a lot of what your tween says can seem irrelevant to you, but it's important that you listen. Kids can tell when you're not listening to them or when you're not paying attention, and this will dishearten them. Whatever your tween is telling you, listen with interest, acknowledge, reply and show enthusiasm. They will remember it the next time you're telling them something and they'll listen to you.

Don't pretend to listen when you're actually doing something else – watching TV, working or trying to rest. When your tween is trying to talk to you, share their feelings or talking about their day, they deserve your full attention. Listen to them, ask questions, engage with them, and give the right reactions when needed. If you are in the middle of something, stop and listen to them for 5 minutes, then excuse yourself and go back to what you were doing. Make a great show of the fact that your tweens have your attention: turn off the TV, turn around to face them, or put your phone down, when you are listening to them.

If you are actually busy and your tween has picked a wrong time, be honest about it: *"I'd love to hear about this, sweetie, but can you tell me about it a few minutes later? I'm in the middle of something very important, but I will only need 10 more minutes, and then we'll talk about what happened at school."* Your tween might be sad at this dismissal, but they'll understand eventually; in fact, they'll actually appreciate the honesty you've shown them instead of the fake attention.

Besides, remember that your tween will imitate your listening skills by watching you interact with them! If you pretend to listen to them while busy with something else, pretty soon that's exactly what they're going to do to you. I'm pretty sure you won't like that! If you want full attention from your tweens when you are talking to them – talking to them about anything, both serious and not-so-serious, you'll need to give them the complete attention they want from you when they're the one talking.

Watch your Tone

Your tweens will start to pick on your tone more than on the words you are speaking. Therefore, whenever you talk to your kids, make sure you are not speaking in an exasperated, angry, frustrated, annoyed or tired tone.

Sometimes, you can't really help it – to be honest, especially when your kids bombard you with questions and accusations the moment you walk through the door. But when you do end up taking a bad tone with your kid, control yourself and apologize, and then repeat in a normal, upbeat tone.

Similarly, refrain from using a whiny tone when you are giving them an instruction or order. Remove any traces of uncertainty from your voice and make it an authoritative one - the type of tone that suits with power and control. When you are setting limits, use a confident tone that no one would want to argue with.

More importantly, when your tween wants to share anything with you – however mundane and ordinary – remove all traces of impatience from your voice. Sometimes, parents sound as if they are waiting for their kids to stop talking so that they can get a word in, and children can pick up on the impatience.

Don't Nag

Nobody likes to be nagged, not even your tweens. When you need them to do something (or not do something), give out your instruction in a firm, authoritative voice, making sure that they have heard. Add the deadline for the task, and if possible, the consequence for not following. Repeat once instead of nagging continuously, using the same authoritative tone, because there's a chance they've forgotten.

The third time, follow up with action. Do what you have promised to do before if they hadn't listened. Don't even hesitate to follow through.

Example:

First instruction: **"This episode only, and then you will turn off the television and start on your homework, because it is time."**

Reminder: **"Has the episode ended yet? You don't get to watch another one tonight. Turn off the television."**

Action: ***turn off the television***

Do this a few times and your kid will know that you mean business. Keep on nagging, and they'll automatically learn to disregard your initial instructions, knowing that there'll be many more to come before you actually take action.

Acknowledge the Good Behaviors

As parents, we sometimes pass out on everything good that kids have done and only comment on the wrong ones or the mistakes. We mistakenly think that our job is to correct our children or to teach them, and that's what we do all the time.

Sometimes, when you see your tweens doing something you've told them to do before, you should acknowledge it with a *"How lovely that you remembered"* or a *"I'm really glad that you remembered"*, or a *"Well done!"*, or just a smile. When your tweens understand that you are acknowledging and appreciating their positive changes, they will start to pay more attention to what you say.

Think of it this way, they listened to you and changed themselves for you, did something without you asking and nagging, and you didn't even acknowledge it. Would that be enough to encourage them the next time? No, it wouldn't. What would encourage them to listen to you and obey your instructions when you see them doing something positive and thank them for it, or at least acknowledge it with a smile.

Respect Them and Get Respect in Return

Parents often fail to recognize this but during the tween years, your children look for more than your affection and love. They need their parents to respect them – respect their right to choose, to speak up, to be heard, to be appreciated for having and opinion, and more. In short, the kind of respect and acknowledgement you have for another individual.

What's the best way for parents to show that you respect your tween? By carefully listening to what they have to say, and not trying to force your ways on them. Every time you shut down an argument with *"We know what's best for you!"* or *"You're not old enough to understand what you want"*, you are making your tween realize you don't respect their wishes, and that will result in them losing respect for you. Any kind of remarks that you make like these – the ones that completely disregard their wishes and needs, you are actually distancing yourself from your tweens. By not respecting them, you are losing their respect. Even when they are your children and you've given birth to them, and taken care of them, you need to respect their individuality.

The most direct way that children show disrespect is by not listening to you; they will disregard your advices, ignore your instructions and disobey your orders. So, the best way to deal with this: *show your tween the respect they need to see from you, and get respect in return.*

Parents thought the teenage years were the most difficult ones for a parent-child relationship, but the tween years, or the pre-teen years as they are also called, aren't much better. During this age, your children will be more reluctant to listen to you, simply because they think they know better. Although this is something extremely frustrating, it's also something to carefully handle. **Too lenient with your tween, and you won't be able to control them later; too strict, they will rebel and oppose you every step of the way.**

Making your tween child listen to you is just one of the parenting challenges you will face during these years. The key is to keep a smooth relationship with them and keep the lines of communication open, to show your tween that you love and respect them, and the rest will, hopefully, follow through.

Chapter 5: Getting a Teenager to Listen to you

Teenagers never listen! Either they are too busy glued to their screens, too wise to listen to anything you have to say, too many homework and projects to deal with, or have too much of a social life to spare you a minute. Whatever the reason, listening to anyone slightly older is completely out of the agenda for them.

And this is not just when you are the parent, but also for teachers, aunts, grandparents and guardians – any adult with a teenager to take care of. To be honest, teenagers can be quite horrid when they want to be, which is most of the time. The teen years can be some of the most trying years of your life if you are a parent.

Why are Teenagers So Difficult?

Ages 13 to 19 – the teenage years, are the most stressful years, both for a child and a parent. The child that has always been so lovable can turn sullen and non-communicative overnight, and that can hurt. A lot. Parents often feel left out and ignored at this age, since their teenage children always seem so busy somewhere else. This can become a point of clash in many families, because parents feel that the children should be more responsive, more involved and more proactive in the home, and this is exactly what teenagers are not.

However, as parents, we need to start thinking of the situation from the point of our teenage children.

The teenage years are not just a time in their lives, it is a special transitional phase when they are leaving behind their childhood and adolescent days to become an adult. They've only just managed to come into terms with all the physical and emotional changes in their body, which has of course been extremely difficult for them. Suddenly, they are required to grow up, make adult decisions and start planning for the rest of their lives.

This is not just in your teen's minds; there are actual hormonal changes that can be seen in their brains. Their brains begin to create a complex situation regarding everything in their lives – their grades, friends and social peers, the pressure to choose a career, sudden differences of opinions from parents, sexual attraction to the opposite (or the same) gender, morals and resolutions, disillusionment about reality, everything. Within a very few years, your children grow up to be fully functioning adults, and the transition is always hard.

Why wouldn't teenagers be difficult, you tell me!

What can you Expect from Teenagers?

If this is your first time handling a teenager, or if your child or children are becoming teenagers soon, you need to know ahead of time what to expect from one.

1. Expect to experience a multitude of emotions within a very short time. Within a 24-hour range, your teenager will show signs of being happy, moody, relaxed, sad, tormented, edgy, agreeable, frustrated, angry and/or devastated.

2. Expect that your teenager child might love you, but they won't particularly like you, any time of the day; the same goes for you, as well.

3. Expect that they'll be blaming everything on their hormones, their luck, or on you.

4. Expect that they'll be on their phones a lot, preferably texting. Expect to receive all your information via texts instead of a conversation.

5. Expect to stock up on junk food, especially chocolates, ice cream and chips. You'll need to buy a lot of food, period.

6. Expect that you'll never be able to guess what mood your teen is in before they open their mouth.

7. Expect that whatever you say will mostly be received in the wrong way, followed by an argument.

8. Expect that you will be tired like you were when they were newborns, surprisingly.

9. Expect no forms of communication from your teenager for a long time, until you initiate a conversation.

10. Expect to hear a lot of *"You'll never understand"* and *"There's no use telling you".*

11. Expect to burst with pride just by looking at your teen, and find them rolling their eyes at your emotion.

Communicating with Your Toddler, Tween, Teen and Older Children – Know How to Get Through to Your Kids

12. Expect to spend a lot of time waiting for them to come home, for a call, for a text or for an answer after you've asked a question.

13. Expect to know the full forms of a LOT of acronyms.

14. Expect them to never have enough clothes (this one is mostly for the teenage girls).

15. Expect to have a lot of patience simply to go through the day.

16. Expect that they'll never want to hug you, even when you know that they need one.

17. Expect for anything that you've never expected.

18. Expect them to sleep a lot and through everything.

19. Expect a lot of talking back and silent treatments.

20. Expect that you don't know how to handle a teenager, because no guideline or manual will be able to help you raise your kid.

Fun aside, a teen child can be your best friend or your worst enemy, or both! You'll actually never know what to expect with a teenager in your home. They can be sweet as honey one minute and depressed the next, and there isn't much that you can do about it, except be supportive and present whenever they need you.

However, one of the biggest problems that you can expect from your teenager is that they'll very rarely want to listen to you. At this age, there isn't much that you need to instruct them about, since a teenager already knows the right ways to do something and what's best for them. You could give them advice and guidelines, but they will not be in the mood to listen to you. Teenagers think they know everything, and there's nothing else than an adult can teach them.

In reality, it is extremely important that you keep the modes of communication open with your teenager, and the effort needs to come from your side. Unless absolutely necessary, teenagers don't often show much enthusiasm in listening to what the adults have to say, but this isn't the right way. Until they are completely adults, teenagers absolutely need to listen to what the parents are saying, and there are some ways that you can make it happen.

Getting your Teenager to Listen

The teenage years are not about your teens listening to you; they are more for you to listen to them. The more thoughtful and understanding you are, the more you listen to their side of the story and take an active (but not too inquisitive) interest in their life, the more attention you are going to get from your teen. Think of it this way: *to get them to listen, you have to learn to listen.*

Here are some helpful ideas and hints for parents on this topic – on getting your teenage child to listen to you.

1. Know Everything That's Going On

You want your teenager to listen to you? First, keep a track of everything that is happening in their life. They won't repeat the same information again so the moment that they say something, memorize the details.

A new friend they mentioned? Something they mentioned they find interesting? A career choice they are thinking about? Someone they had a fight with at school? Some boy/girl at school they like, or they think likes them? A teacher they had a crush on? Some celebrity they admire and follow? Keep everything they've mentioned in your mind and gather as many information as you can about them. Your teen probably won't mention the same things again, but they can appreciate if you remember everything they've told you.

If you remember these tiny, almost unimportant, details – this is something they are going to recognize the value of. It means that you've listened to them talking thoroughly, and in return, there's a small chance they may pay attention to what you say.

2. Don't Rush or Nag

With regular people, repeating something for the third or fourth time can be considered nagging; for teenagers, everything that you say for the second time will be welcomed with an exasperated sigh and eye rolling.

Nagging, repeating, rushing – these things don't work with teenagers. You can tell them to do something as simple as making the bed, and it will take them a few hours to get to it. Teenagers do everything – if they do them – at their own speed and pace. You can't rush them or nag them into doing anything that doesn't appeal to them, not unless you are in the mood for an argument to break out.

Teenagers hate when you nag them, about anything. However, if it is something important that needs to be done immediately, you can remind them about it a second or a third time, but using tricky words.

Example: You've told them to make the bed, but you know they haven't. Instead of reminding them to make it again say, *"Now that you've made the bed, can you bring your dirty laundry down"?* This can be an indirect nudge that will be reminder they need to get on with the job.

Step#2: If that doesn't work, you can ask, in a matter-of-fact, tone: *"Bed done already? Thanks, hun!"*

Step#3: When nothing works and you don't want to whine and nag, say in your most authoritative and serious tone: *"Make your bed right now, I'm not going to say it a second time!"* This is necessary at some point. When your teenager refuses to grow up, you have to order them around like a child.

You can try any of these three techniques, but what you can't do is nag. The more you nag, the less your teenager listens to you, because of course, when you are nagging and whining, you are giving them the power in the conversation.

3. Don't Give Lectures

Your lecturing days are long over! Even younger children don't want to sit down for a lecture, let alone your teenager. Whatever you have to tell them, make it short, concise and to the point. Do not launch into a long (read: boring!) monologue about anything, unless your teen has come to ask you for advice on something.

The more words you use, the less attention you get from your teens. So, whatever you have to say, make it shorter than a Twitter post. Speak as if you are writing a text, because these days, teenagers don't have enough attention span. Whether you are giving an instruction, having a conversation about their future plans, telling them about your day or offering advice, make your sentences short and your speech shorter. Draw them in with questions rather than continuing a monologue no one is listening to; ask their opinions on what you are saying, and ask what they feel about the whole thing.

When the situation arises, you can still give them a 'lecture', but try to make it as concise as possible so that your teen doesn't lose interest in the middle.

4. Don't Compare

If there's one thing that teens (and all children) hate, it is to be compared to someone else, something all parents, knowingly or unknowingly, end up doing.

Whether you are comparing them to their friends, another teen in the neighborhood, your own teenage self, or anyone else in the world, **you are sending one simple message to your teen: _they are not good enough._** It can be that they don't bring in good grades as their best friends do, or that they are not ambition enough as the neighborhood kid who got into a good college, or how they are not well-mannered as you were at their age, or whoever you are comparing your children to – you are not being fair. Every children is different, and you're only hurting your teen by being competitive.

Whenever you compare your teenager to someone you think is being proper or better, you are distancing yourself from your own child. No teenager likes being compared and feeling inadequate, and they are gradually going to shut you off. The more you complain and compare notes, the less they are going to waste their time listening to you.

So, if you feel like your teen is shutting you off, ask yourself: *have I been making them feeling inadequate too much?* Even if that hasn't been on your agenda, parents should never compare their own children with anyone else, because this is something that really hurts them.

5. Don't Criticize or Judge Too Harshly

Between the ages of 13 and 18, there will be a lot of times when your teen will be taking the wrong decisions. Whether it is a phase of bad clothes, a new haircut gone wrong, some new friends you don't approve off, a new hobby that doesn't suit their personality – these bad choices are a part of their growing up.

As parents, you might be bursting to say something or make a comment on their hair or clothes, but what you need to do is to hold your tongue. Unless this is a life-altering mistake that your teen is making, let them. Don't criticize too harshly with comments like *"What have you done to your hair? Are you out of your mind?"* or *"You look ridiculous!"* because that's not the right path to take. Too many judgmental comments or criticisms, your teen will simply stop communicating with you or asking for your opinion.

As I wrote above, unless they are thinking of quitting school, getting a tattoo or mixing with the very wrong crowd, let them make their mistakes. That's how your teen is going to learn to make decisions in life and learn from their own mistakes. Too much interference and criticism, and you can be sure that your teenager is going to stop listening to whatever you have to say very soon.

6. Be Honest

When criticizing, offering an advice or giving an opinion, be as honest as you can. Everyone appreciates honesty, even your sullen, moody teenager. Don't worry about how they are going to take it, but always be honest in your opinions.

When your teenager asks about you at their age, be as honest as possible without giving them any ideas. Don't make yourself up to be absolute angels who had done nothing wrong or made no mistakes in the past, because that is simply not possible. Try to tell them the truth as much as possible, but also add the consequences to your mistakes. Omit what you don't want your impressionable teens to know, but don't lie about the whole thing.

Simply say *"I've made a few mistakes in my life when I was your age, that I am not proud of and that I don't want you to make."*

This will make you sound human to your teen instead of: *"I was responsible at your age and I never made any mistakes. I always listened to what my parents told me to do, and I never disagreed with them or disobeyed them."*

Your kids aren't naïve; of course they'll know you're lying, and lose respect for you. You can't really expect your teenagers to be truthful about what they are thinking or doing when you haven't been honest with them. Your teens will appreciate you being open with them, and they will listen to you instead of shutting you out.

7. Don't Force your Preferences on Them

Your teen is a separate individual from you, and their preferences will of course be different from yours. As the parent, you can't really force them to like what you like, dress the way you dress, watch the movies you like to watch or read the books you read. You can guide them or even suggest your choices, but you can't force them.

Neither should you criticize your teen when they make a fashion statement or a new hobby you don't really understand. When they ask for your opinion, don't start with *"You are crazy to wear something like this; this is completely inappropriate, definitely not something I would have worn, ever!"* or *"Why would you want to do something like this? I would have never taken up this hobby in a million years!"*

Your teenager is not you! You may be the parents but they are their own individuals. They will have interests and preferences that are completely their own and has nothing to do with you. Just because you have taken care of your children forever doesn't mean they have to like and do everything similar to you. Let them make their own choices in life that could be completely different from yours, and be completely neutral when asked for an opinion.

8. Let them Make their Own Future

One of the biggest mistakes that parents make is to assume that their children will follow in their footsteps, and the teenage years are when this starts or becomes most prominent. *"My daughter is going to be a doctor because we are doctors"* or *"Our son has to become a teacher because we are all teachers in our family"* – these kind of ideas may seem simple but are quite harmful to your teens.

When you are automatically planning your children's future, it could mean that you are completely ignoring them or not hearing them in the process. Your children can have completely different ideas from you about their future that you are ignoring because you are planning their futures for them. This is not really an uncommon scenario in many households that can completely turn your teens against you.

If this is something that you have done forever – to disregard your children's choices and wishes because you are set in your ways – it could be one of the biggest reasons your teens don't really communicate or listen to you. Your teen will be ignoring your words because you are disregarding their freedom to choose.

This is not something parents should do. **If you want your teens to listen to you, stop pressuring them to agree to your plans for *their* future**. Listen to your child's wishes about what they want to do with their future, and they will listen to you in return.

9. Treat them Like an Individual

This is one of the most important rules of raising a teenager that you have to remember at all times! You cannot treat your teen as if they are your precious child, always coddling and pampering. Even at age 13, they should be treated like an individual with their own preferences, choices and opinions.

What does this mean, exactly? Treating someone like an adult means you are not going to order for them at the restaurant, simply assume what they will and will not like, choose the books and TV shows they can watch (you can sensor some, of course!), try to show off their talents and skills to guests (which even kids find embarrassing, to be honest), and many other things we do with children. Treating them like an individual also means that you should ask them about changes being made to your house {*"What color do you want your room to be?"*) while planning for a vacation *("Where do you prefer to go?")* and while making plans for the weekend *("Do you have anything planned for this weekend, or do you want to do something with us?")*.

Most importantly, to treat your teen as an individual means never to assume what they want, think or feel, but instead, giving them the respect to ask them.

10. Show Enthusiasm in their Interests

Not just fake interest, but try to take an active interest in whatever your teens like. If they are an avid reader, try reading their favorite books (even when you are not a reader); if they like music, ask if they'll like to learn an instrument. If they like sports, attend any events they are participating in.

Your teens can distinguish between whether you are showing genuine interest in their hobbies or just trying to make conversation. It helps if you are genuinely interested in what interests them; otherwise, simply research into their interests and find out topics to talk about. You can't expect your teens to listen to you unless you talk about something that they find interesting, can you?

Tell them if there's a concert of their favorite band soon, and ask if they want to go; tell them about someone else you know who loved their favorite book. Ask whether they need new running shoes or sports gear if they are athletic, or if they want to visit an exhibition if your child is artistic. Don't be too offended if they are reluctant to share these experiences with you at first; what's more important is that they acknowledge and appreciate your enthusiasm in their interests.

11. Don't Confront Them Too Much

Don't start with a lot of questions the moment they walk in through the door, the instant that they come home from school. You might be doing it with good intention, but they might feel attacked and confronted.

If you bombard your teen with questions like *"What happened in school today?" "Did you do something exciting?" "Did you hang out somewhere?" "Are your friends all good?"* and *"What classes did you have today?"* the moment that they come home, your teens might feel like they are being interrogated. In such scenarios, you might be greeted with complete silence. This is not because your child isn't listening to you, but because they don't want to communicate when cross-examined like this.

If you want answers from your child, you have to start up the conversation casually. Don't put them in the spotlight to know about their life; 8 out of 10 times, they'll be non-committal, ignoring your queries with a *"Fine"* or a *"Nothing to tell"*. Your conversations need to be spontaneous and casual, in a tone that suggests that you are making idle small talk instead of being deeply interested in your teen's day.

Questions like *"So, anything happen at school today?"* sounds much lighter during dinner than if you ask *"How was school? What did you learn? Did you have any fights with your friends?"* the moment you see them after school. Wait until your kid have comfortable a bit to ask about their day; you are more likely to get answers from a teen who have relaxed and already having a conversation with you.

12. Listen to their Side First

This is the age for misunderstandings and misinterpretations. There will be times, pretty sure they happen to everyone, when you will face some complains about your teen from someone else. From the principal, their teachers, classmates, other parents, neighbors or even friends – they can come from anyone. When something like this happens, be sure you are giving your teen a chance to explain before reprimanding them or punishing them.

Before believing someone else or taking away your teen's phone privileges, Internet privileges or driving privileges, listen to their side of the story. The whole thing might be a misunderstanding, someone else's fault or even their own fault, but you should at least give them a chance to explain. Can you really blame them the next time they refuse to listen to your explanations, your side of the story or your decisions?

If you make your judgement based on someone else's accusations, you are indirectly showing your teen that you don't trust them. If you trust them enough, you would have given them a chance to explain themselves, or at least try to. You are not listening to your teen, and in return, they will eventually stop listening to you.

Give them a chance to explain before you pass on the punishment, even if it to admit their guilt and apologize. As parents, our first priority should be our children and we need to trust them, instead of trusting others over them.

13. Be Kind and Empathetic

Our teens can often come with a problem that might seem unimportant and silly to us, but are actually paramount to the children themselves. It can be anything from a pimple to a bullying problem, anxiety about upcoming tests or problems with friends – they are all huge problems in their lives. As the adults of the house, we might be dealing with problems of our own that are colossal compared to theirs, but that's still no reason to underestimate their troubles.

While parents have to deal with financial troubles, health problems, professional competition and other similarly serious problems, the anxieties in our teens can actually seem trivial. However, that doesn't mean their problems aren't worrying to them, and that we have the right to disregard them.

When your teen comes to you with a problem or asks for your advice, always listen. Whatever you are doing and however busy you are, you should always be there to listen and offer support. Whether you can give them a satisfactory solution or not, listen empathetically can always help!

Whatever the problem, big or small, grave or trivial, you should never *joke about it*. Joking belittles the problem your teen is obviously worried about, and judging them would be equally as bad. Saying: ***"You're worried about this little problem? Do you*** *think this is even important enough to lose sleep over?"* or *"When you said you have a problem I imagined something serious, but I see that it is nothing!"* will only guarantee that your teen never comes to you with another problem again.

"I can see why you are worried" or *"That IS a problem. Do you want to know what I would do in your place?"* or *"Yes, I would have been worried too if I were you!"* – these are the appropriate answers to give whenever your teen comes to you with a problem. Take them seriously and your teen will listen to you. They might not like the solutions you offer or even disagree with you, but they will listen.

14. Don't Pester Them

Your teen might not always be ready to talk to you, so don't bother them too much if they are not in the mood. If you ask them a question and they don't reply or give you a non-committal answer, it simply means they are not in the mood to communicate. Don't take this personally even when it may feel rude or debasing; your teen probably doesn't mean to insult you or make you feel bad. They are driven by emotions and at that moment, they don't want to talk.

If you pester them with comments such as, *"I asked you a question and you have to answer it"* or *"I won't stop asking until you've told me what's wrong"*, they are only going to shut off more. The more you harass them, the less chances of them answering you. They might just shut you out completely if they think you are being a nag or a bore.

So, what will be the right path to take? Shrug and say, *"Not in the mood? I can understand. Well, you know where to find me!"* and leave the room. You are the first person your teen is going to seek out when they do want to talk about it and listen, just because you knew to leave the matter alone.

15. Don't Seek out Special Moments

With young children, you need to plan some special times to spend together, but this doesn't work with teens. With teens, you can't really seek out specific time or activities with them, but incorporate some conversations throughout the day. You can ask about their friends when driving them to school, about their hobbies when having dinner together or about their grades while you are watching TV together.

To ask a teen *"Let's plan something together this weekend, just the two of us!"* is probably never going to work (most of the time), because your teen is possibly going to be busy with one thing or another. You have to catch them between chores to have a conversation because that's the only way you can actually get their attention.

Another way to catch your teen would be to ask them along for your chores, like *"Can you come with me to the dry cleaners, please? The load gets too much for me alone sometimes"* or *"Would you mind dropping me off at the dentist please, before you go meet your friends?"* The idea is to spend more with them, with or without a decent conversation; you can talk but your teen will only listen when they are comfortable with you, and that happens only after you've spent some time together.

16. Set Boundaries

Your teenager might be almost an adult, but they still need some boundaries. As long as your dependent child is living under your roof and not legally of age, you can set the time to return home, to stay awake or to come down for meals. Treating them like an individual doesn't mean that they can do anything they want to, whenever and wherever they want to.

Just like children thrive on discipline, your teenager also needs some routines and rules in their lives. As they are old enough, you can even ask them to help with the laundry, dusting, cooking and other chores inside the house, as well as outside the house. Setting boundaries will keep them in check and teach them to be responsible adults in the future.

What does it have to do with making them listen to you, you ask? Well, teenagers will respect and pay heed to a parent who is strict at times instead of one who lets them do whatever they wish to. They may be almost adults, but you will always be the parents/guardians, and they will need to listen to you in the future, as well.

17. Don't Try Too Hard

One piece of important advice: *don't try too hard*. You'll need to be the parent to your child through their teenage years, so don't try to be the best friend. You need to be strict sometimes, ignore their pleas when they want to do something dangerous or make too big a mistake. A friend can't do that, but a parent can be harsh sometime and say *"No!"*

Don't try to dress like they do to become their friend; don't use the slangs they frequently use to seem like 'one of the gang'. You'll get plenty of time to be their friend when they are truly grown up, but you need to be the parent from ages 13 to 19. At this time of their lives, teenagers still need a parent who'll guide and discipline them, not a friend who thinks like them and wants to be like them. You can be friendly with them, of course but it's better not to try and be their friend.

18. Involve them

Finally, a good way of disciplining teenagers would be to involve them in household chores and responsibilities. No matter how busy they are with their studies, extra-curricular activities or in their social life, all teenagers – both boys and girls – need to do their part around the house. It can be start with something as simple as taking out the trash to making breakfast for the whole family at least twice a week, keeping their rooms clean or dusting all the furniture once a week. However, you distribute the chores around your home, parents need to always include their teenagers in the household chores.

When your teenagers know exactly what they need to do around the house, you won't need to repeat the same instructions every day. There'll be no more *"Have you cleaned your room yet?"* or *"Have you taken the trash out yet?"* every day when these tasks are a daily part of their lives, just as important as brushing their teeth or going to school, only to be pardoned when there is an important exam, or when they are ill.

Why is it important that your teenagers should be involved in the household chores? Because these young people are soon about to become adults, and they need to learn about being responsible about their lives. They need to start doing everything for themselves soon, and this is the perfect time to start. Involving them in the housework and letting them know what's exactly expected of them every day means that you won't have to go through the same instructions day after day.

A few days of insisting they finish their chores before leaving for school or before they can sit down for dinner, and your kids will automatically start paying attention to your instructions. But yes, you need to be absolutely strict about it. No *"Don't feel like it? Oh well, this one time maybe; you don't have to clean your room, I'll do it"* for them unless there's a pretty good reason.

There's a thin line between being supportive and being liberal, being friendly and being a chum. You can be as friendly as you can with your teenager, but you also need to be strict at times. Be a friend when they want to go to the movies with their friends, but be a parent with the power to say *"Absolutely No!"* when they want to get a tattoo. **Be supportive when they want to pursue a hobby besides their school, but a parent if they want to drop out of school.**

You can be a friend and a parent to your teenager at the same time, because they are going to need both during this difficult period of their life. Don't be too disheartened when you meet with resistance, rudeness or disapproval from your kids, because they are all a natural part of growing up. Before you know it, your teenage child will understand the importance of having friendly-slash-strict parents in their life, and be grate for everything you've done for them.

Until then, hang on!

Communicating with Your Toddler, Tween, Teen and Older Children – Know How to Get Through to Your Kids

Chapter 6: Communicating with Your Grown-up Children

If you think your older children, after they've officially become an adult in the eyes of law, doesn't need you, you are mistaken again. Sometimes, your grown-up children need you just as much as they did when they were children; maybe they won't need you all the time, but they still need your guidance and support.

After your children go off to college, meet that special someone, get a job, get their own lives away from you – it is completely normal for the parents to lose track of their grown-up kids to some extent. After years of taking care of their family, the parents also deserve a break. In between taking a breather and your kids finding out their identity in the world, you can suddenly find yourself distant from your adult children.

Relationship with your Adult Children

While it is completely normal for your children to become a little busy with their own lives after a certain age, they will always need the love and support of their parents, no matter how old they are. They might not need guidelines or advice, but they still need someone to listen to them, especially when they are facing a grown-up problem.

Some adult children call up their parents at least once every day, while others prefer to text; some of them might visit every weekend, while others want their independence. Every family is unique, as are the relationship between parents and grown-up children. Whether your children call you every day or once a week, whether you see them every week or every month – what's important is that your grown-up children know you are there for them.

After ages 19, your officially adult children won't need you to tell them what to do or how to behave, but they will appreciate the chance to talk to you. At this age, communication with your children is more about listening to them talking about their problems than anything else.

Relationship with your grown-up children can be tough at times. They have their own lives, their jobs, their friends and relationships, and later – their own families, to think about. When your children have grown up, it might be tough for parents to accept that the kids' life doesn't resolve around themselves anymore, or that your children have the capability to make their own decisions.

It is especially the parents who have a harder time reinventing their relationship with their adult children, but it's extremely important that you keep the lines of communication open.

In this chapter, I am going to share some ideas on how to effectively communicate with your grown-up children.

Don't Take It Personally

Every time your child ignores your phone call, postpones a visit or forgets to call you back, don't take it personally. Your adult child isn't required to let you know of their every move, tell you their plans or ask for your permission, especially the ones living on their own. When you can't get a hold of them, they might actually be busy with something important. If you decide to take offense every single time they ignore your call, you will only be hampering the easy relationship between you two.

So, accept that your child has a life of their own, needs their own space and has other people to spend time with. They might be busy, or too tired or they might not want to talk to you at that moment. Instead, if you keep accusing them of not paying you enough attention, or ignoring you on purpose, it's only going to create a rift between you.

Don't Interfere in Everything

Whether your child has only become an adult or well into their 20s, your interfering days with them are long days. You don't need to – rather, you definitely shouldn't – interfere and/or offer council on every single thing that they do. You might have been in control over their decisions at one point of your lives, but parents of grown-up children need to accept that your children are adults now. They have the capability of making their own decisions as a grown-up; even when they make mistakes, they have the competence to pick themselves up.

Parents with grown-up children needs to act more like a wise counsel rather than a control tower. You need to be present and helpful whenever you children ask you for advice and guidance, but not interfere in anything they don't want your help with. Financial trouble, relationship problems, parenting woes – help only when asked!

Don't be Too Judgmental

No one wants to be judged to harshly, or too frequently, even your children. A relationship based on judgment and criticism never prospers. Your adult children will never appreciate it if you are always criticizing them and taking on a negative approach to what's actually their lives.

There are going to be a lot of things that your children want to do differently from you; many times, you might completely disagree with what they think, what they do, and what they plan for their lives. It doesn't matter whether your child is wrong or you are wrong, or if you are both right in your own way, or if it is simply a matter of different minds. The more critical you are about your children, the quicker they'll distance themselves from you, and look for other positive influences in their life.

Be Acceptable

There's every chance your children haven't turned out the way you wanted them to, but that doesn't mean you love them any less, does it? They might have not gone into the profession you envisioned them in, or chosen a partner you don' wholeheartedly approve of, but you can't be very vocal about it. If not exactly ecstatic, you should be at least content about their decisions.

Even your grown-up children, with families and loved one of their own, needs to be secured in your love for them, even when they haven't exactly followed in your footsteps. The only thing that should matter to parents is that your child is happy and content, no matter where they are in life, who they are and what they are. Be acceptable about your child, and they will always feel close to you.

Don't Allow Rudeness

Your child might be a grown-up, but they are still not allowed to be rude to you. Period. You can argue like an adult, have discussions and disagreements, even fights, but they are not allowed to be rude. The moment the argument starts to get heated and your children starts to get rude, put a stop to it. Your children may have grown up to become adults, they still need to be respectful

Neither should you – the parent – be rude to your adult child. You might have taken care of them forever, but you actually have no right to be rude to them just because you are the parent. A grown-up child needs to be dealt with as if they are an individual you know, not someone related to you – courteously and gracefully. Conversations need to be mature and sophisticated, and arguments need to be dealt with logic.

Don't Bring in the "I am Your Mother/Father" Argument

Any discussion, argument or disagreement with your adult child needs to be dealt with as if they are an individual who is not exactly closely related to you. If you put a stop to the discussion with the *"I know best; I am your mother/father"* or the *"I took care of you when you were a baby; you owe me this"* logic, you're leaving your children in a lurch.

With this argument, they are supposed to feel bound to be grateful to you, and agree with everything you say. That's not an adult relationship; instead, you're holding your child captive with emotions and blackmailing them to agree with you. It might work a few initial times, but sooner or later, the adult in your child is going to rebel and break free. From you.

Don't Criticize their Parenting Style

This is one of the most common points of disagreement between parents and older children – parenting styles and techniques. When your grown-up kids are parents themselves, you might not agree with the way they are bringing up their kids, your grandchildren. However, it's not really your place (yes, that's right!) to criticize their parenting style. You can suggest something, give them constructive advice, but not criticize or chide them.

When you think your adult child is making a parenting mistake, start with approaches like: *"Have you tried…?"* and *"Do you think it would be better if you…?"* instead of saying *"You're doing this all wrong!"*

Parenting technique change all the time; what was common and right in your time could be considered outdated in your children's time. Parents usually know their own kids better than anyone else, so there's a chance your own children have your grandchildren figured out better than you have. Draw the line at suggestions and advices, but be sure not to mix in criticisms and disapproval.

Listen More than you Talk

Most of your communication with your grown-up children has to consist of you listening while they do the talking. You need to be the person your adult son or daughter comes with their woes, their problems and their heartbreaks; you need to listen while they lament, rant, cry or show rage. Yes, you do get to talk, but not say something like *"I told you so!" or "I knew this would happen"*. Even when you are thinking something along the lines, don't vocalize them.

Listen when they talk, and only give your opinion when asked for them. Resist the temptation to gloat about how your relationships never failed, how you've never had such problems with your partners, or how your children never talked back to you like theirs do. Your grown-up child wants your support and advice, not to feel bad about themselves.

Remember, you are there to listen, not talk. You've told your children what to do and how to act when they were younger, but they are adults now. They know (mostly!) what they want and what's good for them, and all they need is someone who loves them to listen to them. If your children are trusting you with their problems, the best thing you can do is to listen to them. Unconditionally. Unbiasedly. Non-judgmentally.

Maintain your Boundaries

Your child becoming an adult will create some new boundaries between you. Just like you aren't allowed to read your teenager's diary or eavesdrop on their private conversation, you need to respect the boundaries created by your adult children. If they don't want to be friends with you on Facebook, leave it be instead of pestering them with requests; call them up instead of appearing unannounced to their home.

If there's something your adult kids rather not tell you, leave them be. They're adults now and they will have secrets of their own, however bad that may feel to you. Your grown-up children aren't supposed to share every aspect of their life with you, never mind how liberal or open-minded you have always been. They have their own best friends and partners to share their stories with.

Give them space or privacy when they are in a new relationship and don't directly criticize their choice of partner/spouse. At all times, maintain the minimum boundaries that you would with any other adult not related to you.

Take Yourself Out of the Equation

When your grown-up child wants to talk or asks for advice, be your most neutral self. Take yourself out of the equation and only think about what's best for them, their future and their families. When your adult kid tells you they're thinking of moving, don't think about them moving away from you; consider honestly whether this is a good move for them and give your counsel. When they meet someone special they are serious about, don't think about if you like their choice or not; just think about whether they are happy. When they want to talk to you about their future goals, don't impose the career you had in mind for them.

Every time your kid wants your advice, suggestions or guide, be neutral. Think about them and their happiness instead of yours; keep yourself out of their lives for the moment when you want to help them.

Adult children are your peers, your best friends, your family; they're more than the children you've bought up. Your younger children may have been your responsibilities, looking at you for guidelines, instructions and help, but your adult children only need your love and support.

It's hard to deal with a grown-up child, but you can't let the relationship between you suffer. Be the friend when they need someone to talk to, the counsel when they need advice, and the parent only when they need looking after – that's the best way to be close to your adult children.

Conclusion

There you have it!

Every piece of information I have gathered from my months of research, from reading tons of articles on the Internet and dozens of parenting books, and from talking to all (almost) the moms and dads I know, and some more I made acquaintance of specifically for this book. I had even talked to and gathered ideas from my own parents and grandparents, and other parents in my family.

From toddlers to older children, there are different ways to deal with children of all age. Sometimes, you have to be strict, and sometimes, you have to be their friends; at times, you need to be sympathetic, and others, you need to make sure your instructions are obeyed, at all costs.

Every child is unique, and being an effective parent to them is just as inimitable. Although parents know the best ways to deal with their own children, it is completely normal for them to become overwhelmed at times, especially for first time parents of a willful child. When cornered, we can always end up making a bad parenting choice, something that will affect our relationships with our children for the rest of our lives.

This is what I don't want to happen, something that almost happened to my family. If you've read the Introduction of this book, you'll know how I had suffered with my two children ignoring and disobeying me until I decided to become a better parent. Correction, an effective parent, the type my children will listen to, respond to and engage with. It wasn't an easy journey and it took me months, but finally, I have the loving family I had always dreamed of.

This is how this book came to be, with my goal to help other overwhelmed parents struggling with their children. Everything I know about being an effective parent is in this book, and it would make my day if I can help anyone out there.

All the best with this book, and happy parenting!

Thank you!

Communicating with Your Toddler, Tween, Teen and Older Children – Know How to Get Through to Your Kids

Made in United States
Troutdale, OR
07/15/2024

21255819R00054